HOUGHTON MIFFLIN SOCIAL STUDIES

I Know a Place

Tam Steve Tony Amy Mrs. Gray

I know a place
that's oh, so green
where elephant ears
together lean;
a quiet place
that no one's seen
but me.

Rose Burgunder

Beverly J. Armento
J. Jorge Klor de Alva
Gary B. Nash
Christopher L. Salter
Louis E. Wilson
Karen K. Wixson

I Know
a Place

Letter Carriers: We Deliver! USA 25

Houghton Mifflin Company • Boston

Atlanta • Dallas • Geneva, Illinois • Princeton, New Jersey • Palo Alto • Toronto

Consultants

Program Consultants

Edith M. Guyton
Associate Professor of Early
  Childhood Education
Georgia State University
Atlanta, Georgia

Gail Hobbs
Associate Professor of Geography
Pierce College
Woodland Hills, California

Charles Peters
Reading Consultant
Oakland Schools
Pontiac, Michigan

Cathy Riggs-Salter
Social Studies Consultant
Hartsburg, Missouri

Alfredo Schifini
Limited English Proficiency Consultant
Los Angeles, California

George Paul Schneider
Associate Director
  of General Programs
Department of Museum Education
Art Institute of Chicago
Chicago, Illinois

Twyla Stewart
Center for Academic Interinstitutional
  Programs
University of California—Los Angeles
Los Angeles, California

Scott Waugh
Associate Professor of History
University of California—Los Angeles
Los Angeles, California

Teacher Reviewers

David E. Beer (Grade 5)
Weisser Park Elementary
Fort Wayne, Indiana

Jan Coleman (Grades 6–7)
Thornton Junior High
Fremont, California

Shawn Edwards
  (Grades 1–3)
Jackson Park Elementary
University City, Missouri

Barbara J. Fech (Grade 6)
Martha Ruggles School
Chicago, Illinois

Deborah M. Finkel
  (Grade 4)
Los Angeles Unified
  School District,
  Region G
South Pasadena,
  California

Jim Fletcher (Grades 5, 8)
La Loma Junior High
Modesto, California

Susan M. Gilliam
  (Grade 1)
Roscoe Elementary
Los Angeles, California

Vicki Stroud Gonterman
  (Grade 2)
Gibbs International
  Studies Magnet School
Little Rock, Arkansas

Lorraine Hood (Grade 2)
Fresno Unified School
  District
Fresno, California

Jean Jamgochian
  (Grade 5)
Haycock Gifted and
  Talented Center
Fairfax County, Virginia

Susan Kirk-Davalt
  (Grade 5)
Crowfoot Elementary
Lebanon, Oregon

Mary Molyneaux-Leahy
  (Grade 3)
Bridgeport Elementary
Bridgeport, Pennsylvania

Sharon Oviatt
  (Grades 1–3)
Keysor Elementary
Kirkwood, Missouri

Jayne B. Perala (Grade 1)
Cave Spring Elementary
Roanoke, Virginia

Carol Siefkin (K)
Garfield Elementary
Sacramento, California

Norman N. Tanaka
  (Grade 3)
Martin Luther King Jr.
  Elementary
Sacramento, California

John Tyler (Grades 5, 8)
Groton School
Groton, Massachusetts

Portia W. Vaughn
  (Grades 1–3)
School District 11
Colorado Springs,
  Colorado

ISBN: 0-395-80926-6
  5 6 7 8 -VH- 03 02 01 00

Development by Ligature, Inc.

Acknowledgments

Grateful acknowledgment is made
for the use of the material listed below.
Title and **ii** From "A Boy's Place" from
Summer to Summer by Rose Burgunder.

Copyright © 1965 by Rose Stryon. Reprinted
by permission of the publisher Viking Penguin,
a division of Penguin Books USA Inc.
–Continued on page 160

From Your Authors

This picture shows you how corn grows. In this book you will read about how corn becomes corn flakes. You will read about many people and places, in the country and in the city. The words and pictures will tell you how we work and how we get our food.

Did you see the funny face on the ear of corn above? Some of our pages will make you laugh! All of the pages will help you learn more about how we live and work together. We think you will like your new book.

Beverly J. Armento
Professor of Social Studies
Director, Center for Business and
Economic Education
Georgia State University

Christopher L. Salter
Professor and Chair
Department of Geography
University of Missouri

Louis E. Wilson
Associate Professor
Department of Afro-American Studies
Smith College

J. Jorge Klor de Alva
Professor of Anthropology
Princeton University

Gary B. Nash
Professor of History
University of California—Los Angeles

Karen K. Wixson
Associate Professor of Education
University of Michigan

Contents

Unit 1
School   1

LITERATURE *"The Lion and the Mouse"*   2
adapted from *Aesop's Fables*
by Carol Greene
illustrated by Steve Edwards

Lesson 1 *Friends at School*   4

You Decide *How to Be a Friend*   6

Lesson 2 *Working Together*   8

Think About Helping *Doing Your Part*   12

Think About Maps *Looking Down*   14

Unit 1 Review   18

Unit 2
Town and Country   20

Lesson 1 *Too Much Zucchini*   22

Think About Maps *Flying High*   28

Lesson 2 *The Empty Lot*   30

Explore *A Neighborhood*   34

Lesson 3 *Grandma's Album*   36

Think About Time *When Things Happened*   40

Lesson 4 *Come to the Farm*   42

LITERATURE *A Year in the Country*   46
by Douglas Florian

Think About Farms *Food for You*   52

Lesson 5 *One Little Kernel*   54

Think About the Earth   58
The Earth Is Your Home

Unit 2 Review   62

Unit 3
City and Suburb   64

LITERATURE *"Skyscraper"*   66
by Dennis Lee
illustrated by Susan Swan

Lesson 1 *Catch the Bus*   68

LITERATURE *I Go With My Family*   74
to Grandma's
by Riki Levinson
illustrated by Diane Goode

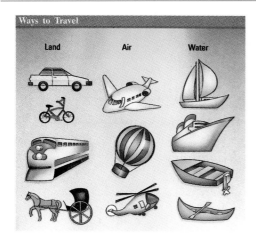

Think About Groups *So Many Ways!* — 82

Lesson 2 *From Kimi's House* — 84

Think About Community *Where You Live* — 88

Lesson 3 *The Bridge* — 90

Think About Why Things Happen
   Asking Why — 96

You Decide *What to Do About Trash* — 98

Lesson 4 *Inside the Factory* — 100

Think About Graphs *Count with Pictures* — 104

Lesson 5 *Night Workers* — 106

Moment in Time *A Fire Fighter* — 110

Unit 3 Review — 112

**Unit 4
All Around the
Big World** — 114

Lesson 1 *Our Country, Our World* — 116

Think About Countries *What Is a Country?* — 122

LITERATURE *The Pledge of Allegiance* — 124
   "America" — 125
   by Samuel F. Smith

Lesson 2 *Across Canada by Train* — 126

LITERATURE *"Trains"* — 130
   by James S. Tippett

Think About Graphs *Count with Bars* — 134

Lesson 3 *A Letter to Mexico* — 136

Explore *A Post Office* — 140

Lesson 4 *From Harbor to Harbor* — 142

LITERATURE *"Tugs"* — 146
   by James S. Tippett

Unit 4 Review — 148

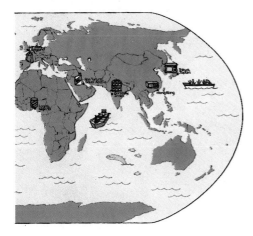

**Information
Bank** — 151

Atlas — 152

Geographic Glossary — 156

Glossary — 157

Acknowledgments — 160

Charts, Diagrams, and Timelines

*These pictures give you facts about the people, places,
and things you are studying.*

Timeline of Grandma's Life	40	Sam's New Friends	134
Timeline of a Plant's Life	41	Days I Traveled	135
How the Corn Grows	55	A Letter Goes to Mexico	137
Ways to Travel	82	Goods From Other Countries	142
From the Factory	104	Our Mail	150
Our Toys	105		
My New Friends	134		

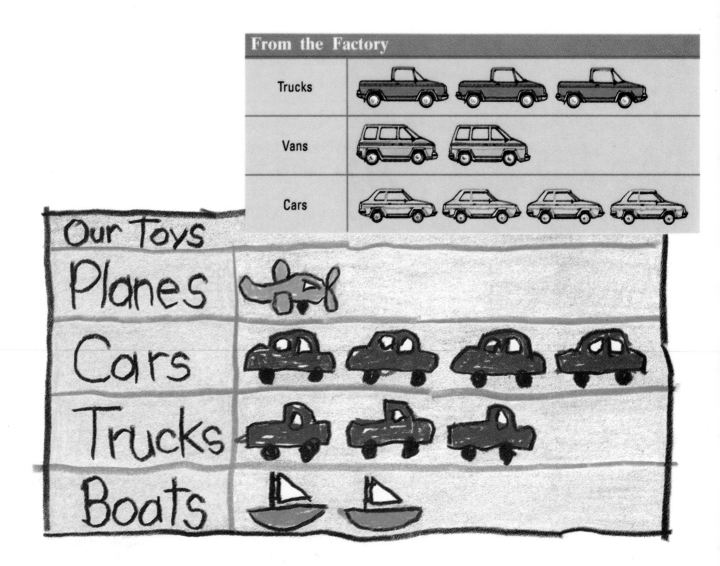

Maps

Each map in this book tells a story about a place.

Classroom	15, 16
Desk	17
Table Top	19
The Town	29
My Neighborhood (a)	30
My Neighborhood (b)	32
My Special Places	87
The City Long, Long Ago	91
The City Long Ago	93
The City Today	95
Our Country	116
Our World	120

Sam's Trip Across Canada	126
Where Anita's Letter Goes	136
Illustrated World Map	144
The United States	148
Mexico	148
United States, Canada, and Mexico	149
The World	152
The United States	154

Starting Out

This is your book.
Let's get to know it.

The number tells you
which lesson it is.

The title tells you
what the lesson is about.

Read the question.
Think about the question
as you read the lesson.

This is a word
you will learn
in this lesson.

LESSON 5

One Little Kernel

Here I am, one little kernel of corn.
The **farmer** calls me "seed corn."
Here I go into the planter.

THINK

Where does the
corn that you eat
come from?

Key Word

farmer

The planter puts all of us seeds in the ground.
It's dark down below, but cozy.
And I am going to grow!

54

See the corn grow.
Pictures in your book
will help you understand
the lesson.

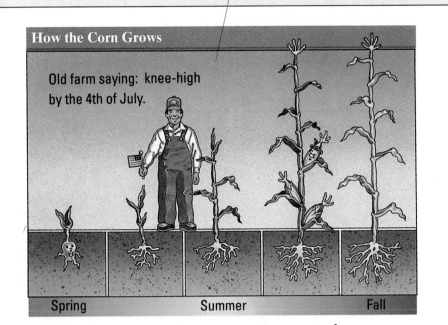

How the Corn Grows

Old farm saying: knee-high
by the 4th of July.

Spring   Summer   Fall

Here is how the corn grows.
First it is just a sprout.
But soon it is a tall plant.

Look, I'm an ear!
I grew on the plant.

I have lots of kernels now.
Here comes the picker!

The ear of corn
is a drawing.
The drawing is not real.

The farm is a photo.
The photo is real.

Drawings and photos
help you learn.

55

Moving On

Pictures and words work together.
Together they help you learn.

Many kernels grew from just a few!
Here we are being put into a truck.
Now the farmer will sell us.

Which is the drawing?
Which is the photo?
Which is real?

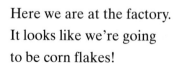

This is the page number.
It helps you
keep your place.

Here we are at the factory.
It looks like we're going
to be corn flakes!

56

I was right.
Here I am at the store.
Buy me! Buy me!

I'm in a pretty bowl!
I'm in a shiny spoon!

GULP!

The lesson tells you
how things happen.
First the corn grew.
Next the corn
went to market.
What happened last?

REVIEW

1. Where does the corn that you eat come from?
2. What does a farmer do?
3. Where did your breakfast come from?

At the end, review
what you have read.
The answers
to the questions
are in the lesson.

57

Learning More

You can learn in many ways.
Special pages in the book
help you to learn more.

Do you like to explore?
This page tells you how.

This page tells you how
to put things in groups.

EXPLORE

A Neighborhood

In the last lesson Charles made maps of his neighborhood. You can make a map of the neighborhood around your school. You can put model buildings on your map.

Get Ready

1. Talk about the place you want to explore. What streets and buildings will you see?
2. Get things for drawing and for making model buildings.

Find Out

1. Go outside your school. Look all around. What streets do you see? What do the buildings look like?
2. Draw pictures of what you see.

34

THINK ABOUT GROUPS

So Many Ways!

The girls in the last story went to Grandma's house. Each girl went a different way.

There are many ways to travel. There are ways to travel on land and in the air and on water. You can put the ways in groups. What groups do you see below?

Ways to Travel

Land   Air   Water

82

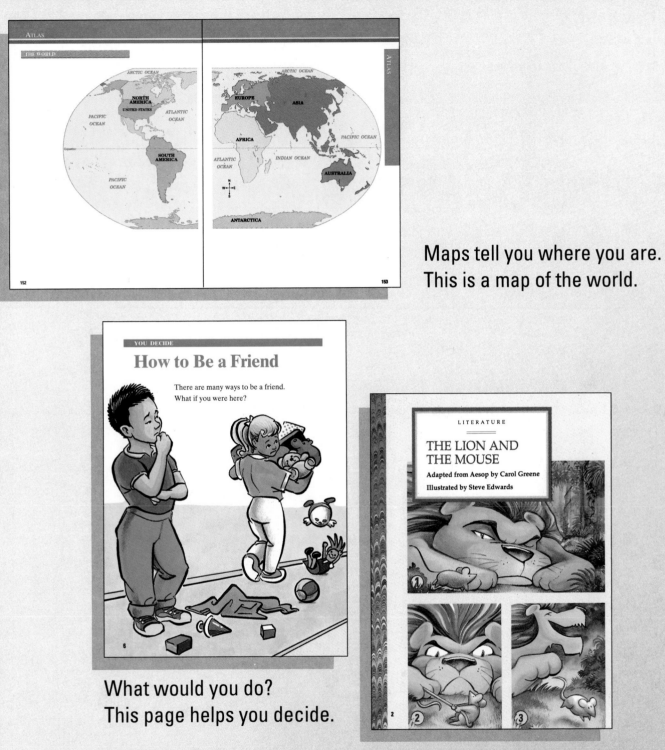

Maps tell you where you are.
This is a map of the world.

What would you do?
This page helps you decide.

Your book has stories, too.
Stories help you learn.

Unit 1

School

Friends at school
Are big and small.
Friends at school
Are best of all!

THE LION AND THE MOUSE

Adapted from Aesop by Carol Greene

Illustrated by Steve Edwards

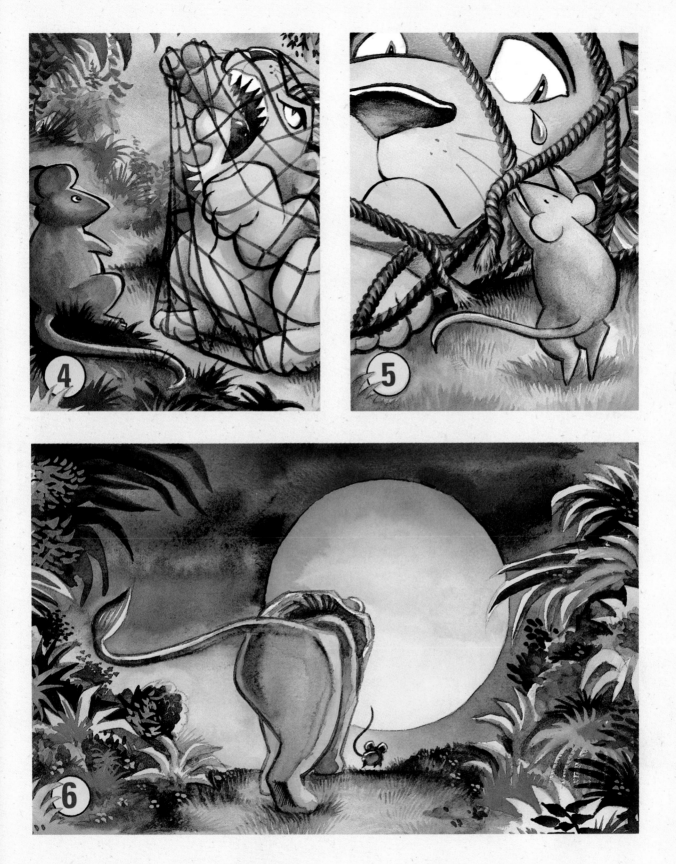

Friends come in all sizes.

Friends at School

Who are
your friends
at school?

Key Word

friends

1

2

violet

yellow

4

3

5

REVIEW

1. Who are your friends at school?
2. How can you be a friend?

How to Be a Friend

There are many ways to be a friend.
What if you were here?

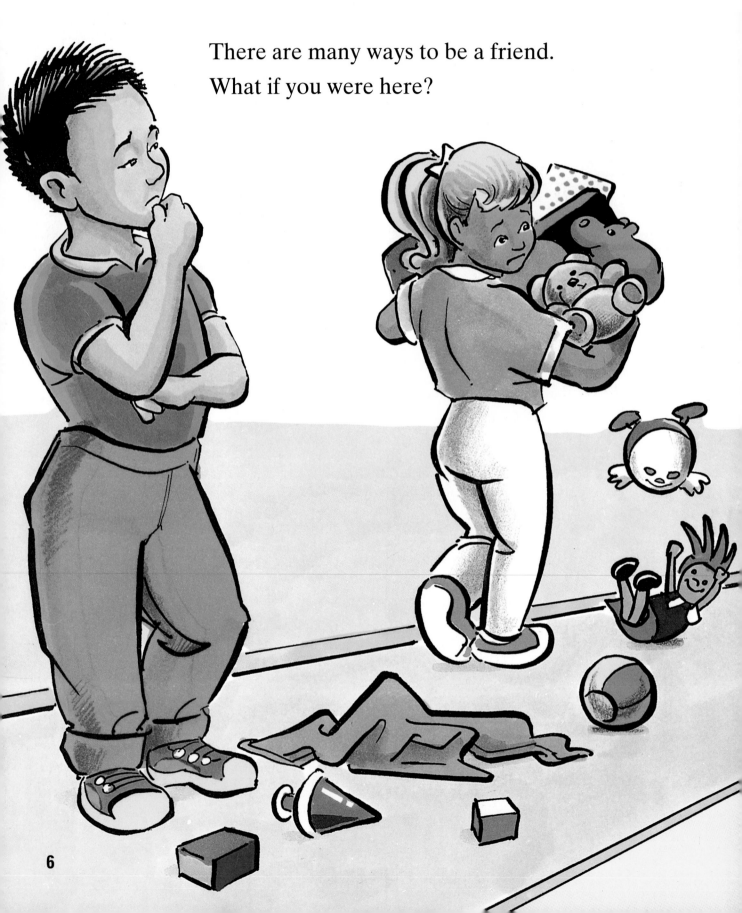

6

You could help in these ways.

How would
you help?
Why?

7

Working Together

Tam   Steve   Tony   Amy   Mrs. Gray

At school

1 The boys and girls will bring treats on Friday.

2 What will they bring?

3 Tony's dad says to take paper plates.

4 Steve's grandma says to take plates, too.

5 Tam's mom and dad have lots of plates.

6 Amy's mom has popcorn. What will happen next?

Friday at school

7 There are lots and lots of plates!

8 The girls and boys are hungry!

9 Mrs. Gray says the boys and girls can try again.

10 The class works **together.**

The next Friday

11 Tam tells her mom that she needs grapes.

12 Tony's dad gives him some carrots.

13

REVIEW

1. How does a class work together?
2. Why were there too many plates?
3. Why do people work together?

Doing Your Part

You saw how Mrs. Gray's class worked together. Everyone helped. What happens when people help? What happens when people do not help?

Helping

Not Helping

Helping

Not Helping

Helping   Not Helping

Helping   Not Helping

Helping means doing your part. It means thinking about other people. Helping makes people happy. How do you help?

Looking Down

Imagine that this is your school.

What if you could float up?

How would the
room look?

This is a map of
the room.
A **map** shows how
a place looks from
above.
Can you tell what
these things are?

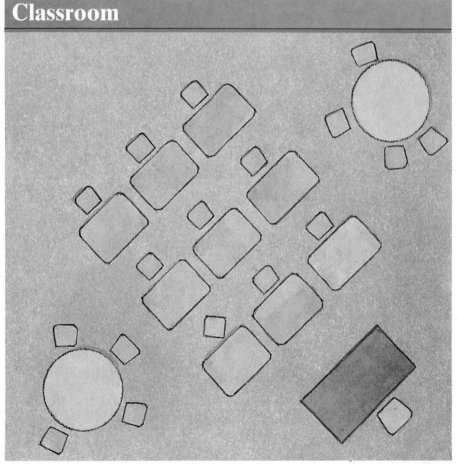

Classroom

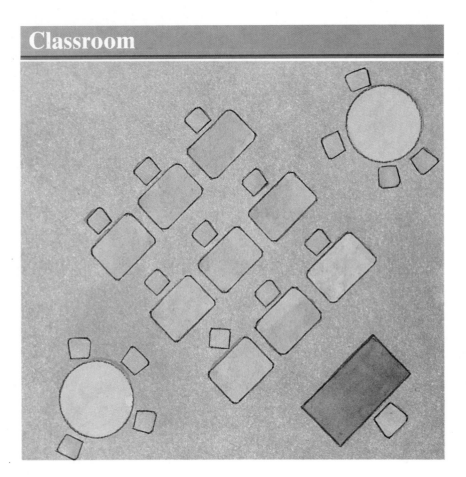

Classroom

A map can have a title.
It tells what the map shows.
What is the title of this map?

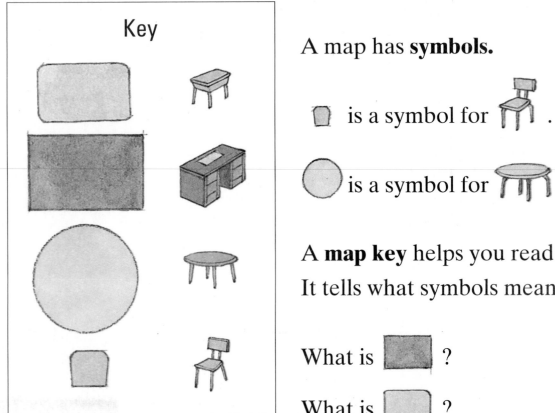

Key

A map has **symbols.**

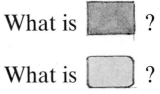 is a symbol for a chair.

is a symbol for a round table.

A **map key** helps you read a map.
It tells what symbols mean.

What is ?

What is ?

Try It!

1. Put some things
on your desk.

2. Look down.

3. Make a map.
Give it a title.

4. Make a map key.

Unit 1 Review

Words

Tell what two pictures go with each word.

friends

together

Ideas

Draw two people who help you at school.
Tell how they help.

Skills

Look at the map. Answer the questions.

Table Top

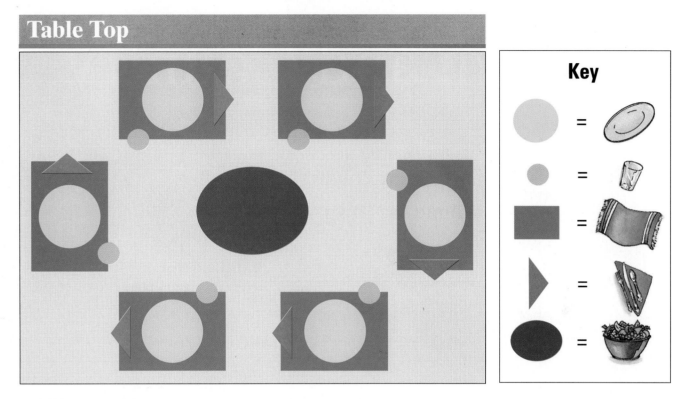

Key

1. What does the map show?

2. What is ⬤ ?

3. What is ▶ ?

4. How many ▮ are on the table?

Activity

What do the children in your class like best about school? How can you find out? Work together with two or three others. Make a plan to find out. Tell the class your plan.

Unit 2
Town and Country

Look around the country.
Look around the town.
What can you see
When you look down?

Too Much Zucchini

THINK

What kinds of places are in a town?

Key Word

town

"Help!" says Dad. "The zucchini is over the dog house!"

"There is too much zucchini!" says Mom.

Mike and Jenny will take some to friends in their **town.** You can come, too.

Mike and Jenny go to see Uncle Pete.
Uncle Pete lives down the street.

"We have too much zucchini,"
says Jenny. "Do you want some?"

"Oh, thank you," says Uncle
Pete. "I can make zucchini jam."

Free Zucchini

23

Next Mike and Jenny go to Sue's.
Sue makes food for people in the town.

GIFTS

Sue's Cafe
Home Cooked Food

Smith Shoes

NTRY FAIR
KT. 6-9

TOWN HALL

Free Zucchini

"We have too much
zucchini," says Mike.
"Do you want some?"

"Oh, thank you," says
Sue. "I can make
zucchini cake."

24

Then Mike and Jenny go to the fire house.
The fire fighters help keep the town safe.

"We have too much zucchini," says Jenny.
"Do you want some?"

"Oh, thank you," say the fire fighters.
"We can make zucchini stew."

Now Mike and Jenny go to the feed store. The store has food for animals. It has tools and seeds for farms, too.

"We have too much zucchini," says Mike.

"I know what you mean," says Mrs. Hill. "I have too many rabbits. Do you want some?"

Free Zucchini

26

At last Mike and Jenny go home.
All the zucchini are gone. But the
wagon is very full.

"Help!" say Mom and Dad.
"Too many rabbits!"

Free Zucchini

1. What kinds of places are in a town?
2. Draw someone who works in a town.

Flying High

What if Mike and Jenny could fly above their town and look down? Everything would look different!

This picture shows how a town might look from above. Places look smaller from far away.

Here is a map of the town. The map
shows how places look from above, too.
Find things in the picture. Then find them
on the map. What color is the lake on the map?
What color is the land?

The Town

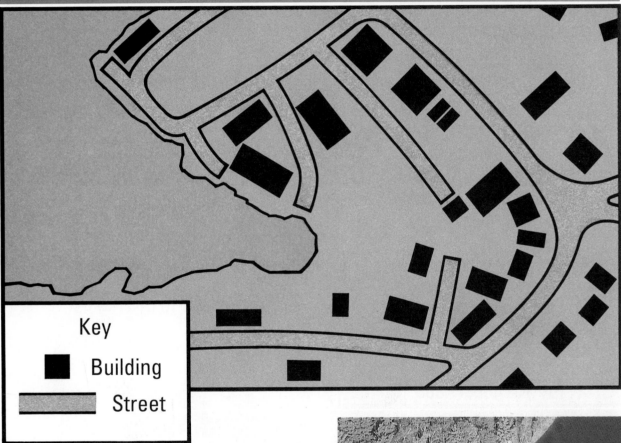

Key

■ Building

▬ Street

Try It!

Draw a map of this picture.
Use colors to show land
and water. Make a map key
to show the boats.

The Empty Lot

How does a
neighborhood
grow?

Key Words

neighborhood

grow

My name is Charles. Guess what happened in my **neighborhood!**

My neighborhood has houses and people. But last year I didn't have a friend to play with. There was an empty lot across from my house. Sometimes I played there by myself.

My Neighborhood

My House

My Street

The Empty Lot

Then my neighborhood started to **grow.**

One morning a loud machine came to the lot. It dug out some of the trees. It made a big, square hole in the ground.

I was sad because some trees were gone. My dad said, "Wait and see. Something good may happen."

Soon I saw what was happening. There was going to be a new house!

I wondered who would live there. I still missed the empty lot.

My dad said, "Wait and see. Something good may happen."

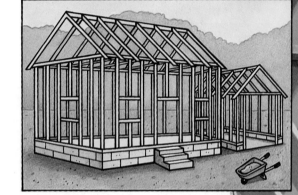

My Neighborhood

My House

My Street

The New House

Now there is a new house in the neighborhood. I have two new friends. Today we planted a tree together.

Dad was right.
Something good *did* happen!

REVIEW

1. How does a neighborhood grow?
2. What things are new in your neighborhood?

A Neighborhood

In the last lesson Charles made maps of his neighborhood. You can make a map of the neighborhood around your school. You can put model buildings on your map.

Get Ready

1. Talk about the place you want to explore. What streets and buildings will you see?
2. Get things for drawing and for making model buildings.

Find Out

1. Go outside your school. Look all around. What streets do you see? What do the buildings look like?
2. Draw pictures of what you see.

VILLAGE SCHOOL

Move Ahead

1. Draw the streets of the neighborhood on a very big sheet of paper.
2. Make models of your school and other buildings.
3. Put the models on the big paper.
4. Trace around each model to make a big map.

Grandma's Album

THINK

How does
a family grow?

Key Word

family

Grandma shows Emily her **family** album. "You were a little girl like me," says Emily.

"Yes," says Grandma. "Here I am when I was a baby. Then I got bigger and bigger, just like you."

"What was it like then?" asks Emily.

"My family lived right here in this town," says Grandma. "The town was smaller then. I had a mother and a father and a big brother named Jimmy. Look, here I am with Jimmy."

"Did you have fun way back then?" asks Emily.

"Oh, yes!" says Grandma. "Here I am
with my toys and my pets and my friends."

"I like those funny cars," says Emily.

"And then you grew up!" says Emily.

"Yes, I grew up and had my own little girls," says Grandma. "Then my little girls grew up. One of them is your mother. So now I am your grandma."

"And I'm glad you're my grandma," says Emily.

REVIEW

1. How does a family grow?
2. Find out what it was like when your grandparent was your age.

When Things Happened

Grandma told about her life. She told about events in the order they happened. You can show the order of events by making a timeline.

A **timeline** helps us see when things happened. To make a timeline, think about what happened first and what happened next.

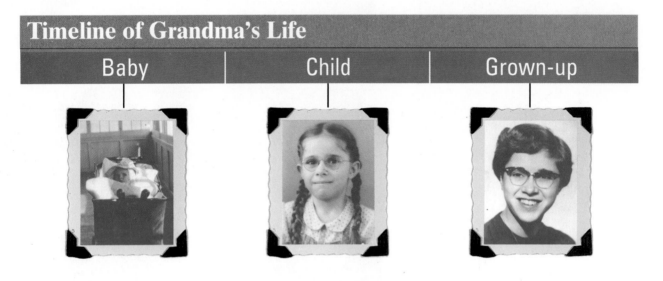

Timeline of Grandma's Life

| Baby | Child | Grown-up |

Look at the pictures below. How would you put them on a timeline? What happens first? What happens next?

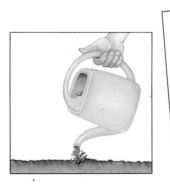

Here are the pictures again. Now they are on a timeline. Why is it easy now to see what happened first and what happened next?

Timeline of a Plant's Life

Seedling	Leaves	Buds	Flowers

Try It!

Make a timeline of your life.
Think of three important events.
Show the events in order.

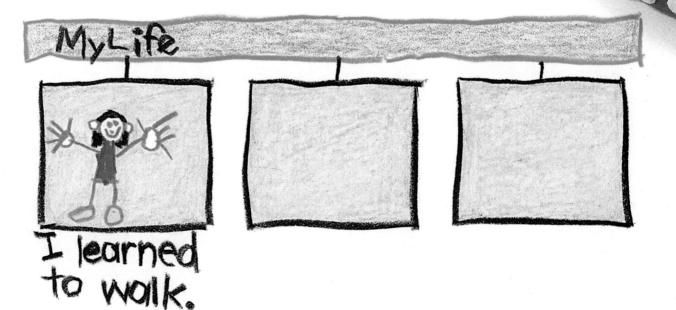

My Life

I learned to walk.

Come to the Farm

Come to the **farm** in the springtime.
Touch the new buds on the twigs.
Smell the earth as the plow goes by.
Look at the baby pigs.

THINK

What can you
see and do
on a farm?

Key Word

farm

Come to the farm in the summer.
Feel the breeze blow through your hair.
Eat fresh corn and ride a horse.
Go to the country fair.

Come to the farm in the autumn.
See the harvest and smell the hay.
Wave at the kids on the big yellow bus.
They are off to school today.

Come to the farm in the winter.
Feed the animals safe inside.
Wrap up well in your warmest clothes.
Then run to the pond and slide.

REVIEW

1. What can you see and do on a farm?
2. Why do children who live on farms ride school buses?
3. Draw what you would like to do on a farm.

You read about seasons on the farm. Now see what happens there each month of the year.

LITERATURE

A YEAR IN THE COUNTRY

Written and Illustrated by Douglas Florian

January

February

March

April

May

June

July

August

September

October

50

November

December

The year is over—
and a new year begins.

Food for You

There are many different kinds of farms.
Some farms are big, and some are small.
Foods come from many kinds of farms.

Raising milk cows

Picking oranges

Catching catfish

Working in a rice field

Feeding hens

Growing pineapples

A farm is a place where people grow plants or raise animals. Think about all the food you eat. Almost all of it comes from farms.

One Little Kernel

Here I am, one little kernel of corn.
The **farmer** calls me "seed corn."
Here I go into the planter.

THINK

Where does the
corn that you eat
come from?

Key Word

farmer

The planter puts all of us seeds in the ground.
It's dark down below, but cozy.
And I am going to grow!

How the Corn Grows

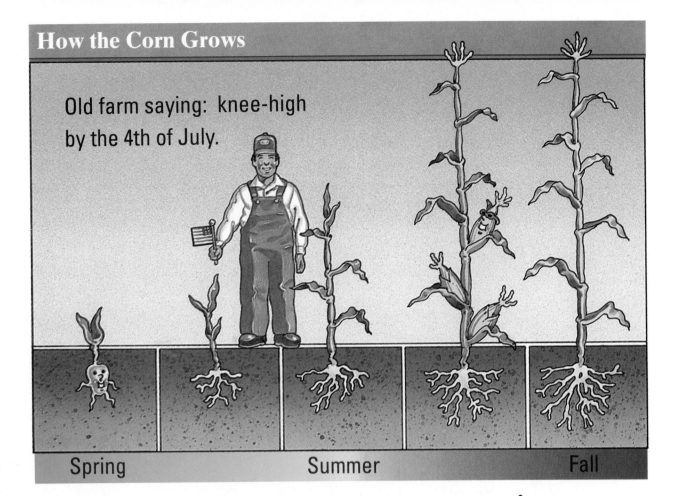

Old farm saying: knee-high by the 4th of July.

Spring   Summer   Fall

Here is how the corn grows.
First it is just a sprout.
But soon it is a tall plant.

Look, I'm an ear!
I grew on the plant.

I have lots of kernels now.
Here comes the picker!

Many kernels grew from just a few!
Here we are being put into a truck.
Now the farmer will sell us.

Here we are at the factory.
It looks like we're going
to be corn flakes!

I was right.

Here I am at the store.

Buy me! Buy me!

I'm in a pretty bowl!

I'm in a shiny spoon!

GULP!

1. Where does the corn that you eat come from?
2. What does a farmer do?
3. Where did your breakfast come from?

The Earth Is Your Home

Some people live on farms. Some people live in towns. Some people live in other places. But we all live on the earth.

Way out in space, the earth looks like this.
All you can see are clouds and oceans and land.
You can't see people or houses. But they are
still there.

Have you ever seen a model of the way the
earth looks?

A **globe** is a model of the earth. You can see land and oceans on a globe.

The **North Pole** is a place on the earth. It is near the top of a globe.

The **South Pole** is a place on the earth, too. It is near the bottom of a globe. Find the poles on a globe.

North Pole

South Pole

When you move toward the North Pole, you go **north.** Put your finger on a globe. Move your finger toward the North Pole. On the real earth, this way would be north.

Going north

When you move toward the South Pole, you go **south.** Put your finger on a globe. Move your finger toward the South Pole. On the real earth, this way would be south.

Going south

Try It!

Make a picture of a globe. Show land and water. Show the North Pole and the South Pole.

North Pole

Unit 2 Review

Words

What word goes with each picture?

family

farm

farmer

neighborhood

town

Ideas

1. Draw two windows. In one window, draw what you might see in a town. In the other window, draw what you might see on a farm.
2. Tell about some of the people and places in your neighborhood.

Skills

1. This is how a park looks from above. Make a map of the park.

2. Look at the mixed-up pictures. Tell what happened first, next, and last.

3. Look at the globe. What does a globe show?

4. Which way is the ✈ going?

5. Which way is the 🚂 going?

North Pole

South Pole

Activities

1. Make a picture of your family. Work with your class to make a book that shows all the families.

2. Work with a partner to make a big poster. On the poster, put pictures of foods from farms.

Unit 3
City and Suburb

What is a city?
Do you know?
Trains and trucks
And cars on the go;
Big tall skyscrapers
Up in the air;
But, most of all, people;
People live there.

Some big cities have tall buildings called skyscrapers. Read a poem about a skyscraper.

LITERATURE

SKYSCRAPER

Written by Dennis Lee

Illustrated by Susan Swan

Skyscraper, skyscraper,
Scrape me some sky:
Tickle the sun
While the stars go by.

Tickle the stars
While the sun's climbing high,
Then skyscraper, skyscraper
Scrape me some sky.

Catch the Bus

It's morning in the big **city.**
Where are all the people going?
What will they do today?

Hop on the bus!
Hurry! Find a seat.
Let's take a look at the busy city.

THINK

What can you
see and do
in a city?

Key Word

city

Look out the bus window.

You can see people hard at work.

These workers are building a new hospital.

How does their work help others?

Look, the man has on roller skates!
What a funny sight! He is in a hurry.
He has to be at the bank by nine o'clock.

Stop the bus!
People want to get off
at the shopping mall.
Some people buy things.
Some people just look.
What can you find in a mall?

Beep! Beep!

The driver honks.

The woman is running to catch the bus.

She works at the ball game.

Hurry! Hurry!

The children are having fun. They are looking around the big city. Next, they are going to the ball game. What else can you do for fun in a city?

REVIEW

1. What can you see and do in a city?
2. How do people have fun in a city?
3. How is a city different from a town?

You have learned many things about cities and the people in them. Now go back in time to New York City long ago. Read a story about five girls who visit their grandmother in the city.

LITERATURE

I GO WITH MY FAMILY TO GRANDMA'S

Written by Riki Levinson

Illustrated by Diane Goode

My name is Millie and
I live in Manhattan.
I go with my family
on a red and
yellow bicycle

to Grandma's.

My name is Bella and I live in Brooklyn.
I go with my family on a golden
yellow trolley

to Grandma's.

My name is Carrie and I live in Queens. I
go with my family in Papa's white wagon

to Grandma's.

My name is Beatie and I live in the Bronx. I go with my family on a dark blue train and a dark green train

to Grandma's.

My name is Stella and I live
on Staten Island. I go with
my family in Papa's big car
on a red and white ferry
across the water, to the city

to Grandma's.

So Many Ways!

The girls in the last story went to Grandma's house. Each girl went a different way.

There are many ways to travel. There are ways to travel on land and in the air and on water. You can put the ways in groups. What groups do you see below?

Ways to Travel

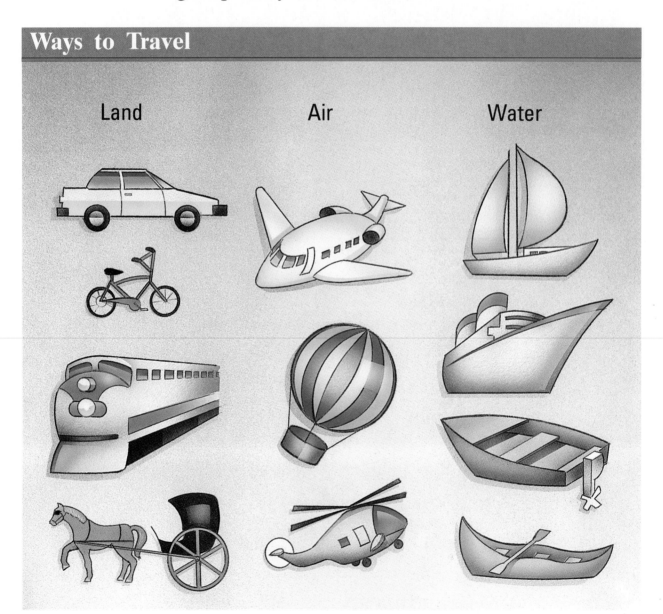

Land   Air   Water

These things are also in groups. Look at each group. Why are the things together? What would be a good name for each group?

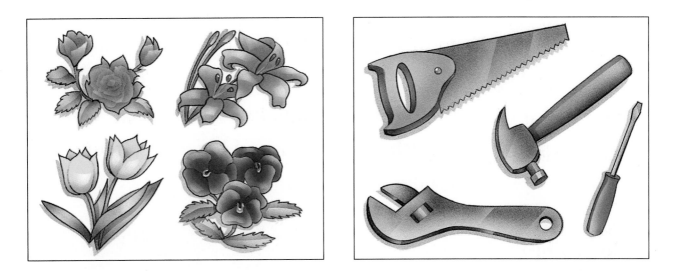

Which things below go together in one group? Name each group.

Try It!

1. Draw things to do on a farm.
2. Draw things to do in a city.
3. Make two groups.

From Kimi's House

Hello. My name is Kimi. My family lives in this house. We live in a suburb called Greenwood. Some suburbs look like towns. Some suburbs look like small cities. But a **suburb** is always near a big city. Greenwood is near a big city called Cook City.

My dad works in an office
in Greenwood. He makes maps.
I like to make maps, too.

My mom works at the
Science Museum in Cook City.
Here she is at work.

I go to school here in Greenwood.
I play kickball here in my suburb, too.

Sometimes my family goes to the Cook City Zoo. I like the big cats the best.

Sometimes we have fun at Greenwood Park. We can walk there from our house.

I like my suburb and the city, too.

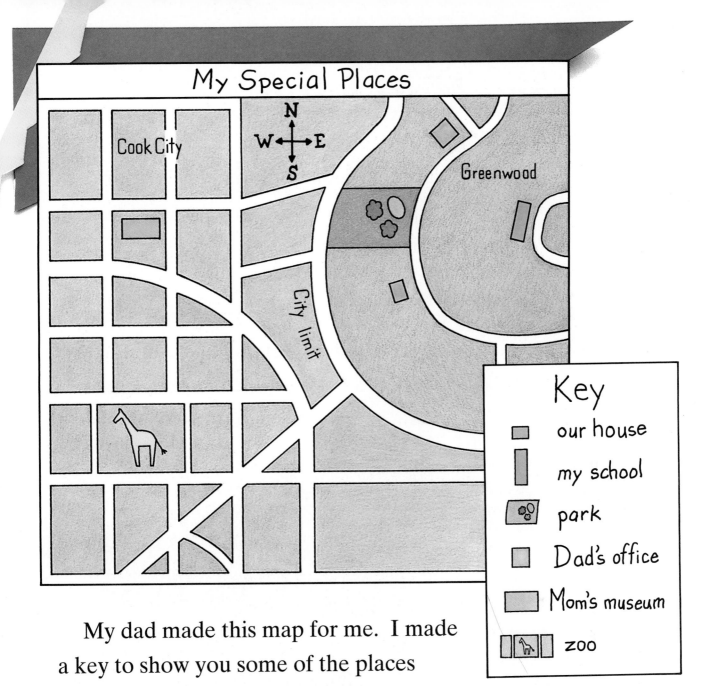

My dad made this map for me. I made a key to show you some of the places I like to go.

REVIEW

1. What kinds of places are in a suburb?
2. How is living in a suburb different from living in a small town?
3. What do you like to do where you live?

Where You Live

You have learned about the places where groups of people live. Each of these places is a kind of **community.**

Your neighborhood is a very small community. It is just the people and buildings near your home.

A town is a small community, too. It is away from any big city. A town has more than one neighborhood.

A suburb is a community near a city. A suburb may be large or small. It may have many neighborhoods, or just a few.

A city is a large community. It has many, many people. It has many neighborhoods.

A community is a place where people live. What kind of community do you live in?

The Bridge

How do cities get so big? How do they get so busy? A town can grow and **change** into a city. Let's see how it happens.

THINK

How do cities change?

Key Words

change

link

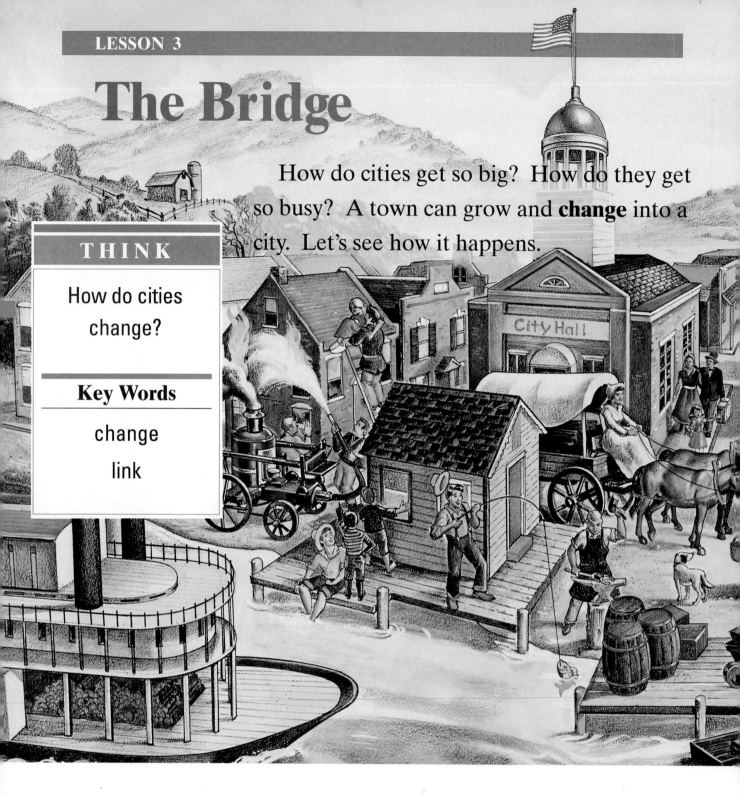

Once there was a town by a river. Roads went from this town to other towns and farms. People walked or traveled by horse and wagon. There were no roads over the river. People needed boats to cross the river.

Then the people had a good idea. They would build a strong bridge. It would be a road over the water. The bridge would be a **link** to other places. How would the bridge help the town change into a city?

The town got bigger and bigger. It became a
city. Cars crossed over the busy bridge. Trains
did, too. Many boats traveled up and down the
river. The first planes flew to the city. The city
had more links to other places.

The City Long Ago

Some things looked the same as before. Many
things looked different. The city had more people.
It had more places to live and work. What other
changes do you see in the city?

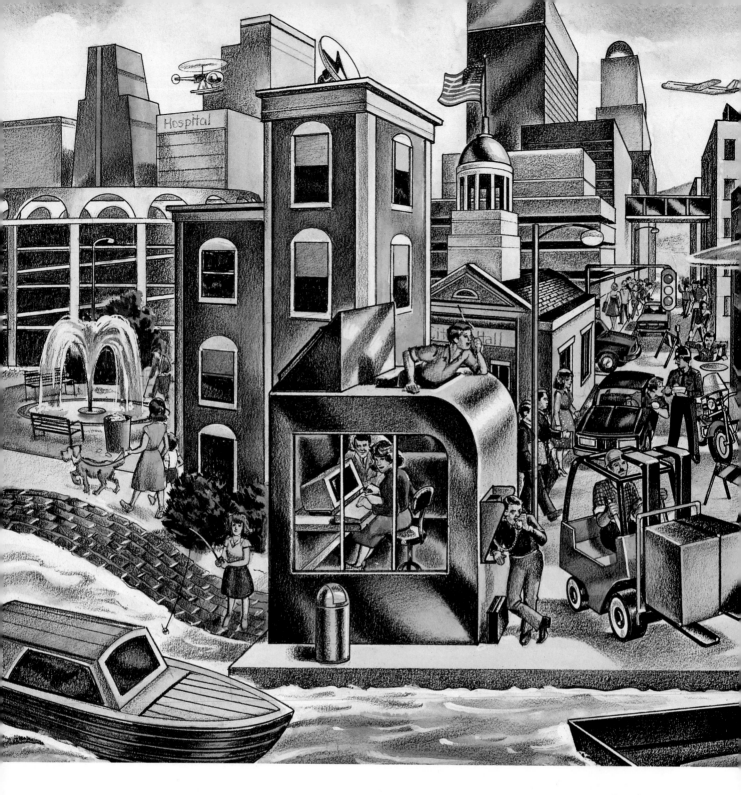

Here is the way the city looks now. The bridge is old, but it is still strong and busy. It is a link to the suburbs and to many other places. What are other ways that people and things can come to the city?

The City Today

REVIEW

1. How do cities grow and change?

2. How are cities linked to other places?

3. How is your home linked to other places?

Asking Why

When something happens we like to know why.

In the lesson about the city, many things happened. Roads and a bridge were built. Why? People needed a better way to get from place to place.

Look at what happened below.

Why was the girl surprised?

This picture also shows something that happened.

Now look at the two pictures below.
One picture shows why the milk spilled.
Which picture shows why?

Try It!

1. Think of something that happened at school.
2. Draw what happened.
3. Draw another picture to show why.

What to Do About Trash

Many people live in cities. Other people live in the suburbs or in the country. Everywhere people live, people throw things away. Things people throw away are called trash.

People can decide where to put trash. Look at the set of pictures. Which way is better? Why?

Throwing trash on the ground

Putting trash in a trash can

Some trash can be used again. Look at the
sets of pictures. Which way is better? Why?

Throwing cans away

Saving cans to recycle

Recycle Here

Collecting paper to recycle

SAVE PAPER

Throwing paper away

Inside the Factory

THINK

What do people
do in a factory?

Key Word

factory

Many cities have factories. A **factory** is
a place where things are made. What do
people do in factories? Let's look inside
a factory that makes cars and vans.

Each new car or van begins with a plan, called
a design. People use the design to make parts.

Body parts are made of metal.
This one looks like a van!

Not all factory work is done by people.
Robot arms put the parts together.

What is missing? The van needs tires and a
motor. Motors are made of metal, too.

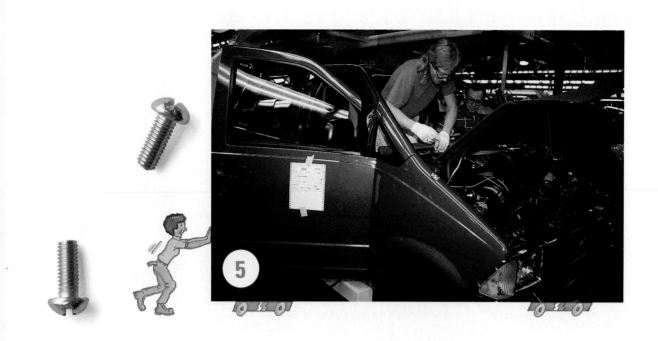

Now the motor is in. Then two workers put cloth and plastic on the inside.

The van is almost done! Will it work?
People will test it to be sure.

Look at all the cars and vans from the factory!
What will happen to them now?

REVIEW

1. What do people do in a factory?
2. What are vans made of?
3. What do you have that was made in a factory?

Count with Pictures

These just came from a factory.

Count the trucks. Count the vans and cars.

You can show how many there are of each kind. You can make a picture graph. A **picture graph** shows how many of each kind.

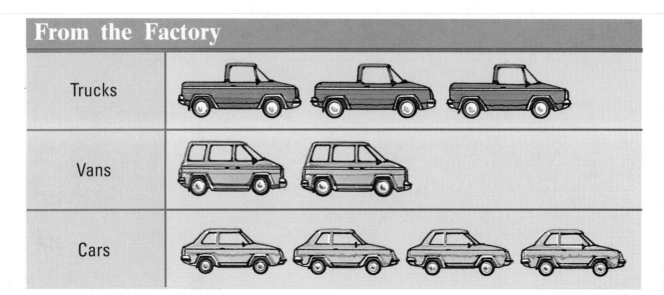

From the Factory	
Trucks	
Vans	
Cars	

Charlie and Tiffany made a picture graph. They lined up their toys and counted them. They showed how many toys were in each group.

How many trucks do Charlie and Tiffany have? How many boats do they have? Which kind of toy do they have the most of?

Try It!

1. Find out what kinds of pets the boys and girls in your class have.
2. Find out how many they have of each kind.
3. Make a picture graph.

Night Workers

THINK

What jobs are done at night?

Key Word

jobs

City

In the morning the city
Spreads its wings
Making a song
In stone that sings.

In the evening the city
Goes to bed
Hanging lights
About its head.

Langston Hughes

taxi driver

Not everyone in the city goes to bed at night.
Let's look at people who work while you sleep.

reporter   editor

press operator

Daily Globe
Newspaper

Bakery

baker

NEWS

While some people sleep, others are busy at their **jobs.** In the newspaper office, workers get the paper ready for the next day. At the bakery, workers make fresh bread and rolls for breakfast.

What other night workers do you see?

doctor

nurse

doctor

security guard

Hospital

AMBULANCE

Toy Town

paramedics

police officer

Sometimes people are sick or hurt at night. So the hospital is always ready. What would happen if the hospital had no night workers? What other night workers can you find?

cleaning crew

artist

Open 24 hours
Hal's Diner

COMPUTER
STORE

fire fighter

waiter

cashier

cook

1. What jobs are done at night?
2. How do night workers help people?
3. Draw a picture of a night worker that you have seen.

A Fire Fighter

When: **Midnight**

Where: **The city**

What: **A fire fighter makes sure the fire is out.**

air tank

helmet

air mask

suit

boots

110

Our fire fighter is a special night worker.
Find out more about the things he uses.

The **helmet** keeps the fire fighter's head safe.
The long back part protects his neck.
The front part keeps heat from his face.

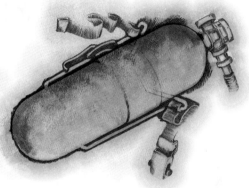

The **air tank** is full of clean, safe air.
A hose takes the air to the mask.

The **air mask** helps the fire fighter breathe in smoky places. When he has it on, he breathes loudly. He sounds scary, but he is a friend.

The **suit** keeps the fire fighter safe from hot fires. The yellow stripes make it easy to see the fire fighter in the dark and smoke.

The tall **boots** keep feet safe from nails and glass. They won't slip on wet floors.

Unit 3 Review

Words

change
city
factory
jobs
link
suburb

What word goes in each blank?

1. A bridge is a _____ to other places.

2. Vans are made in a _____ .

3. A _____ has big, tall buildings.

4. A _____ is a community near a big city.

5. People work at many kinds of _____ .

6. When cities grow, they _____ .

Ideas

1. How is a suburb different from a town?

2. Which things are made in a factory?

Skills

1. Where do you find the things in the box?
Name the groups they go in.

2. Look at the pictures. Answer the questions.

Why is the cat afraid?   Why are the girl's feet wet?

Activities

1. Work with three or four others to save cans for a week. Make a graph like the one below. Show how many cans you get each day. Use your graph to answer these questions.

- On what day did you get the most cans?
- How many cans did you get on Tuesday?

2. Work with your class. Make a book about people who do jobs where you live.

Unit 4

All Around the Big World

Where would you go
If you could go
Out in the big, wide world?

What would you see
If you could be
Out in the big, wide world?

Our Country, Our World

THINK

What is special about our country?

Key Words

country
state
flag

The United States of America is our **country.** It is the land we live in. The United States has 50 **states.** All the states together make our big country.

The map shows the United States in green. Thin dark lines on the map show where the states are.

Most of the states are close together. Two states are far away from the others. These two states are Alaska and Hawaii. What is the name of your state?

PACIFIC OCEAN

N
W E
S

CANADA

UNITED STATES

ATLANTIC OCEAN

MEXICO

Our country has a special **flag.**
It is the flag of the United States
of America. Our flag has 50 stars.
The 50 stars stand for the 50 states.

Our Flag

How bright our flag
against the sky
atop its flagpole
straight and high!

How bright the red,
the white, the blue,
with what they stand for
shining through,

More meaningful
as years go by . . .
how bright, how bright,
the flag we fly.

Aileen Fisher

Our World

The world is a very big place. In it are many countries. Look at the map. The color green will help you find the United States. The dark lines show the other countries.

Edward, Canada

Tracy, United States

Carlos, Mexico

Paulo, Brazil

Claire, France

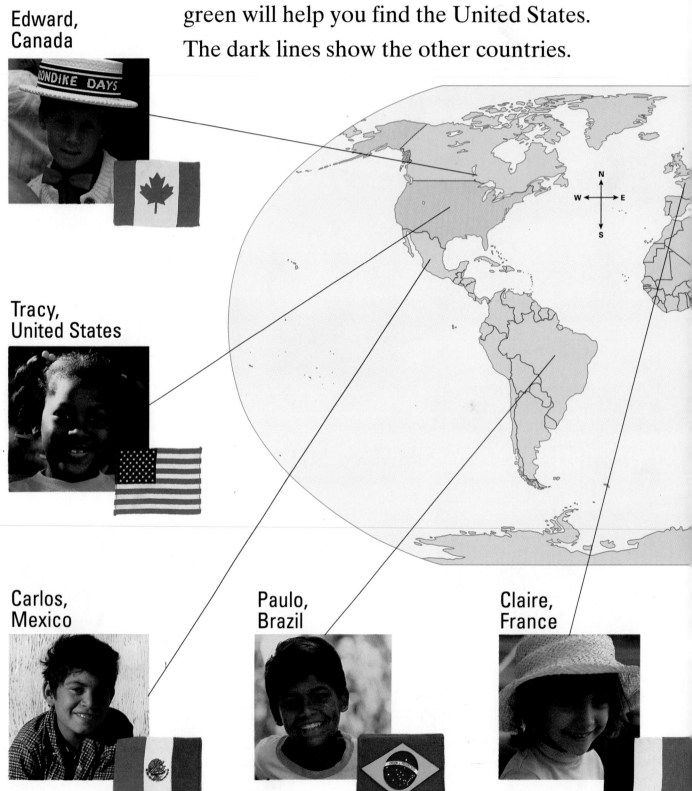

Many people live in the United States.
Many people live in other countries, too.
We are the same in some ways and different
in other ways.

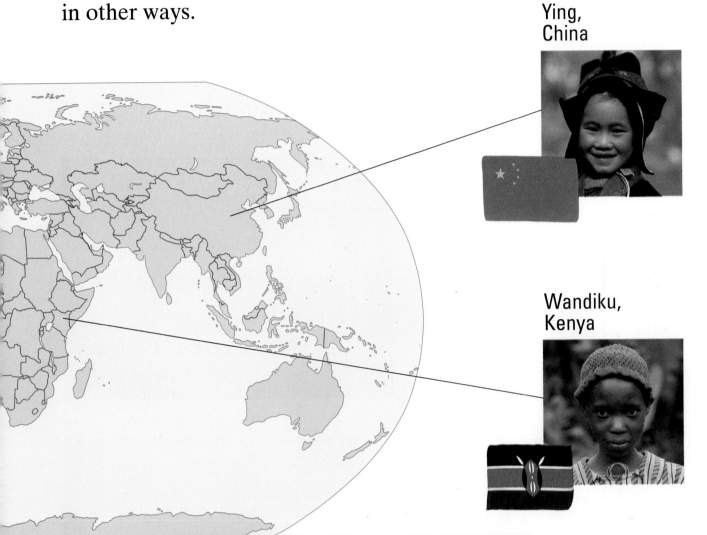

Ying,
China

Wandiku,
Kenya

REVIEW

1. What is special about our country?
2. Tell something about your state.
3. Look at the countries on the world map.
   Which two countries are closest to the
   United States?

What Is a Country?

The United States is a big country. It has a lot of land. It has many kinds of people.

Look at the pictures of our country. What kinds of people live here? What does the land look like?

A country is the land and
the people who live there. The
United States is just one country. There
are almost 200 countries on the earth!

Look at a globe or a big world map to see
all the countries in the world.

THE PLEDGE OF ALLEGIANCE

I pledge allegiance to the flag of
the United States of America
and to the Republic for which it
stands, one Nation under God,
indivisible, with liberty
and justice for all.

AMERICA

Written by Samuel F. Smith

My country 'tis of thee,
Sweet land of liberty,
Of thee I sing.
Land where my fathers died,
Land of the pilgrim's pride,
From every mountain side,
Let freedom ring.

My native country, thee,
Land of the noble free,
Thy name I love.
I love thy rocks and rills,
Thy woods and templed hills,
My heart with rapture thrills,
Like that above.

Across Canada by Train

Sam lives in the United States. He and his family went by train to cities in Canada. **Canada** is the big country just north of the United States. Sam's map shows the way they went.

What is special about Canada?

Key Words

Canada

language

What Sam wrote:

We are going to Canada Wow!!!

Sam's Trip Across Canada

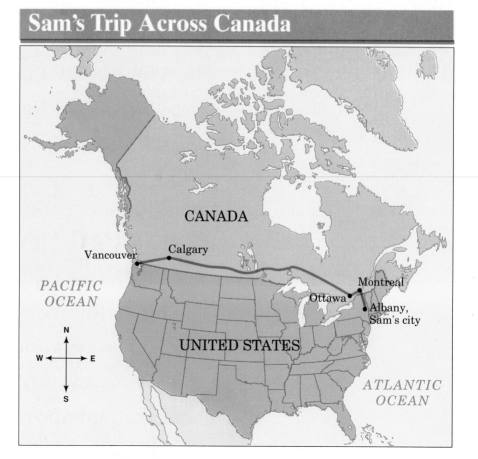

CANADA

Vancouver   Calgary

Montreal

Ottawa

Albany, Sam's city

PACIFIC OCEAN

UNITED STATES

N
W   E
S

ATLANTIC OCEAN

What Sam wrote:

Different things
about Canada:
1. Two languages
2. money
3. The flag

In Montreal, Sam saw a new word on a big stop sign. The word was written in the French **language.** Many people in Canada speak French. Many others speak English. Some people speak both languages.

Sam's mom gave him some Canadian money. He bought a small flag of Canada. Then he made a picture of the flag.

ARRÊT STOP

127

Then the train went to Ottawa. Sam and his family saw Mounties there. Mounties are Canadian police.

Sam bought a carving in a gift shop. It was made by an Inuit artist. The Inuit are among the first people who lived in Canada.
Next, Sam took the train to Calgary. There he saw the biggest rodeo in the world.

What Sam wrote:

I saw some Mounties.

I got an Inuit carving.

I went to a big rodeo!

Vancouver was Sam's last stop. There he watched a soccer game. Canadian children are not very different from children in the United States. Many children in Canada swim in the summer and skate in the winter. We do many of the same things.

Sam will never forget his trip to all the special places in Canada!

REVIEW

1. What is special about Canada?
2. What would you like to see in Canada?
3. What would you show to a visitor from Canada?

You read about Sam's train trip to Canada. Now read about trains long ago.

LITERATURE

TRAINS

Written by James S. Tippett
Illustrated by Frances Flora Palmer

Over the mountains,
Over the plains,
Over the rivers,
Here come the trains.

Carrying passengers,
Carrying mail,
Bringing their precious loads
In without fail.

Thousands of freight cars
All rushing on
Through day and darkness,
Through dusk and dawn.

Over the mountains,
Over the plains,
Over the rivers,
Here come the trains.

Count with Bars

Sam made new friends in Canada. Some of them speak only English. Some of them speak only French. Some speak both languages. Sam made a picture graph to show this.

A **bar graph** also shows how many of each kind. Count the blue squares in each bar to find out how many. How is a bar graph different from a picture graph?

Sam's New Friends

Only English						
Only French						
Both						

Sam wanted to show how he traveled.
He made a bar graph. It shows how many days
he went by train, by car, or by bus.

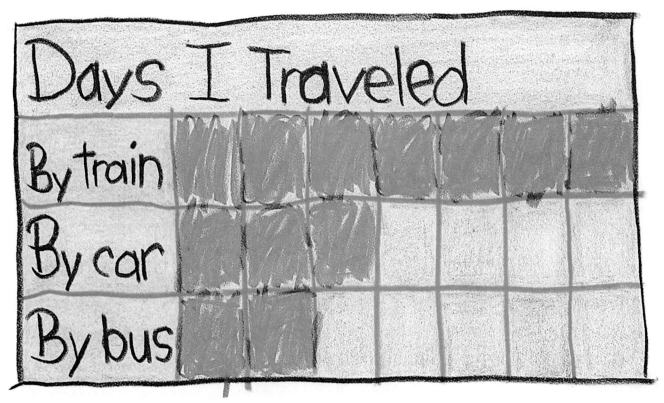

1. How many days did Sam take a bus?
2. How many days did Sam ride in a car?
3. Which way did Sam travel most?

Try It!

1. Find out how your classmates get to school.
   - How many ride a bus?
   - How many walk?
   - How many come by car?
   - Did any travel another way?
2. Make a bar graph to show this.

A Letter to Mexico

Hi! I'm Anita. I'm sending a letter to my cousin, Pablo. I live in the United States, but Pablo lives in Mexico. It takes about a week for a letter to get from me to Pablo.

Mexico is the country just south of the United States. What do you know about Mexico?

Where Anita's Letter Goes

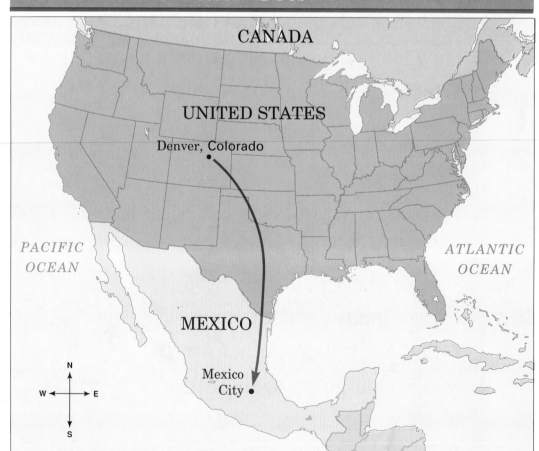

My mom works for the **post office.**
She told me how my letter would go.

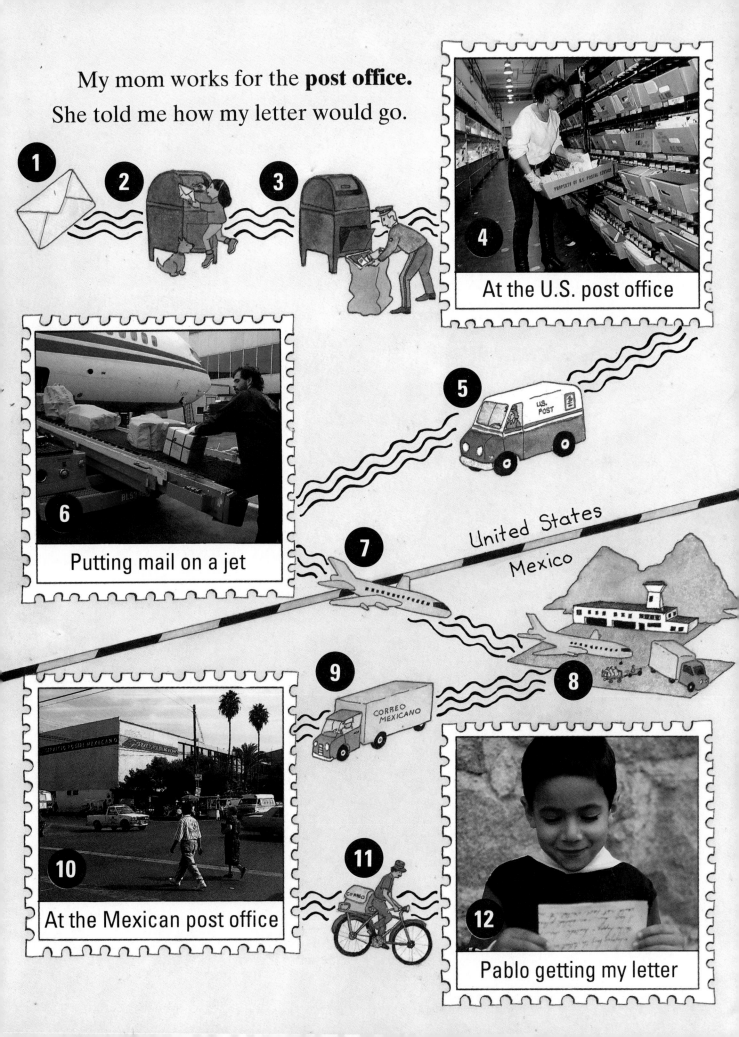

At the U.S. post office

Putting mail on a jet

United States

Mexico

At the Mexican post office

Pablo getting my letter

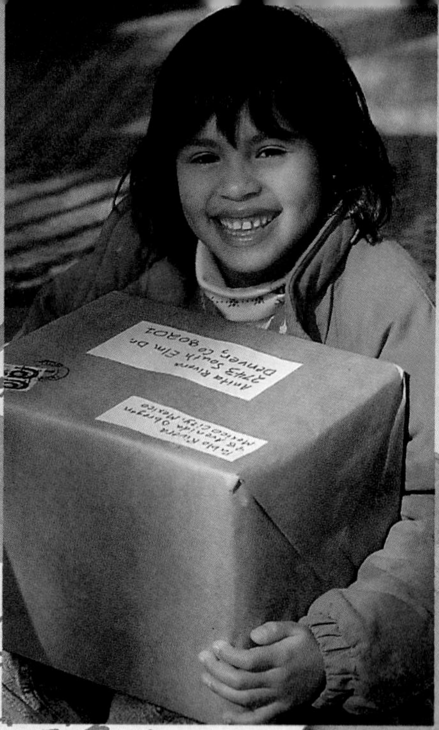

Pablo sent something back to me! Not just a letter, but a package! Look at what Pablo sent me!

El cumpleaños de Spot

¡FANTASTICO!

¡¡NUEVA IMPORTADAS
ELASTICOS PARA
COLAS DE CABALLO

EL BANCO DE MEXICO S.A.
CINCUENTA PESOS

Mexico's flag and the flag of the United States look different. Their money looks different, too.

That game looks like fun. Pablo has a nice family, just as I do. I guess Pablo and I are different, and the same, too.

People in Mexico speak Spanish. Here's one word you can say: *amigo*. (That's Spanish for *friend!*)

REVIEW

1. What is special about Mexico?
2. Where is Mexico?
3. How do letters get from place to place?
4. What would you send to someone in Mexico?

A Post Office

In the last lesson Anita sent a letter to Mexico. You can find out more about what happens to a letter.

Get Ready

1. Talk about how you think a letter gets to another person. What do you think happens at the post office?
2. Get paper, pencils, crayons, and boxes.

Find Out

Look at the pictures. See three things that happen to a letter.

A mail carrier collects the letter.

Workers sort letters to see where each letter goes.

Another mail carrier delivers the letter.

Move Ahead

1. Make a post office in your classroom.
   Have a place to collect and a place to sort.
   Have a place to deliver, too.
2. Choose workers for each job. Take turns.
3. Write letters to your friends in class.
   Use your post office to send the letters.

From Harbor to Harbor

Things that are made and sold are called **goods.** This house has some things that were made in other places far away. These goods came across the oceans on ships. Look at the names of the places the goods came from.

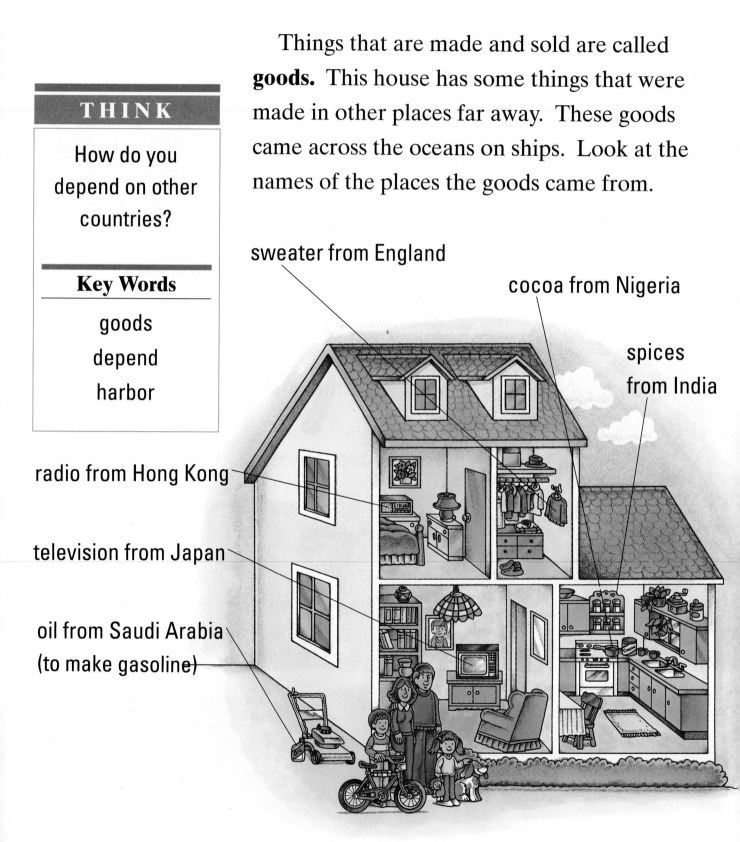

sweater from England

cocoa from Nigeria

spices from India

radio from Hong Kong

television from Japan

oil from Saudi Arabia (to make gasoline)

Why do some goods come from other places?

Some countries do not have all the things the people need. Countries **depend** on other countries to get what they need. The countries buy goods from each other.

Hong Kong Harbor

How do the goods get to our country?

Goods are loaded on ships in a harbor. A **harbor** is a place where ships can dock. In a harbor, ships are safe from storms and big waves. What do you think happens next?

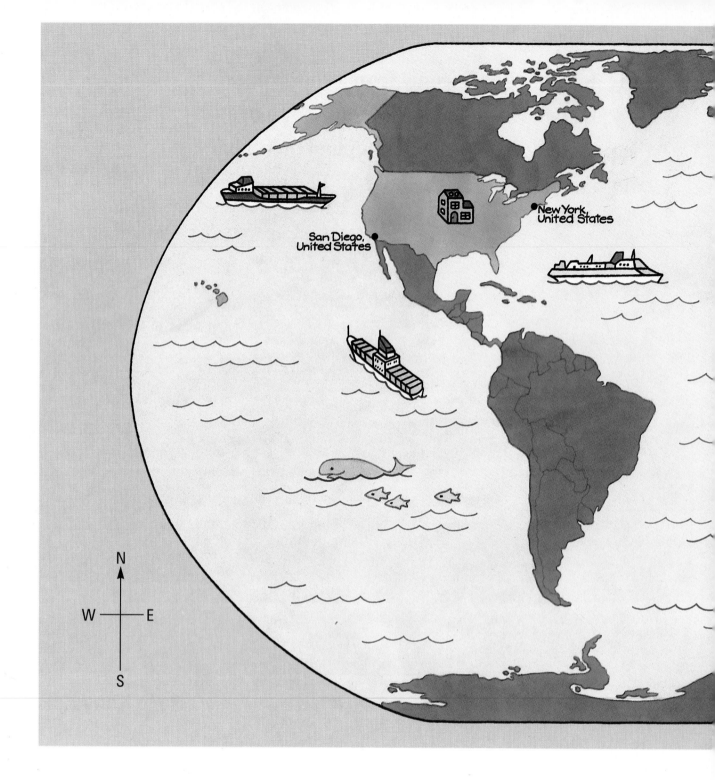

The ships go across the ocean to a harbor in our country. Then the goods are unloaded. Some of the goods get to your house. You depend on other countries for many of the things you have.

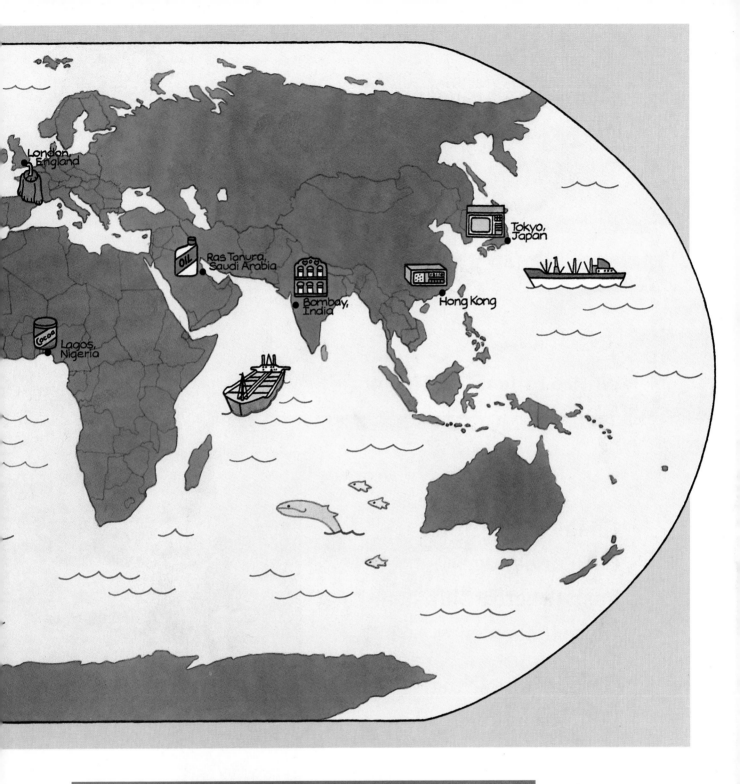

London, England

Ras Tanura, Saudi Arabia

Bombay, India

Tokyo, Japan

Hong Kong

Lagos, Nigeria

1. How do you depend on other countries?

2. Why are harbors important?

3. What do you have from another country?

A busy harbor is full of ships and boats. Read about what a tugboat does.

LITERATURE

TUGS

Written by James S. Tippett

Chug! Puff! Chug!
Push, little tug.
Push the great ship here
Close to its pier.

Chug! Puff! Chug!
Pull, strong tug.
Drawing all alone
Three boat-loads of stone.

Busy harbor tugs,
Like round water bugs,
Hurry here and there,
Working everywhere.

Unit 4 Review

Words

Look at each picture. Tell which word answers each question.

Canada
country
depend
flag
goods
harbor
language
Mexico
post office
state

1. Is this a **country** or a **harbor?**

2. Is the country in yellow **Canada** or **Mexico?**

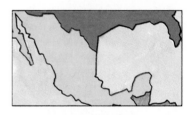

3. Is this a **state** or a **flag?**

4. Is this a **post office** or a **language?**

5. Is this a **harbor** or **goods?**

Ideas

1. Look at the map. Tell which country is the United States. What country is just north of the United States? What country is south?

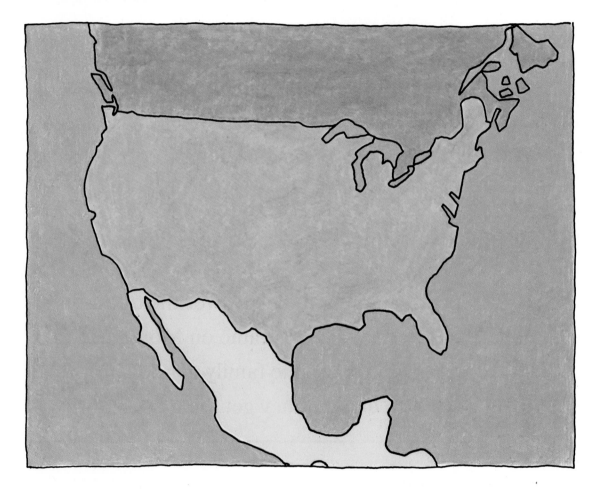

2. The lessons showed three ways that people, mail, and goods can travel to other countries. What are the three ways? Draw a picture of each one.

3. What is a harbor? Why is it important?

Skills

Anita wanted to show how many letters her family got. She made a bar graph.

Look at Anita's graph. Answer the questions.

- How many letters came on Monday?
- Which day did the family get no letters?
- Which day did they get the most letters?

Activities

1. Make a class book about how you depend on other people and places. Make pages for:

   your family   farmers

   your school   factories

2. Work with a partner to make a flag that stands for your school.

Information Bank

Atlas	152
The World	152
The United States	154
Geographic Glossary	156
Glossary	157

THE WORLD

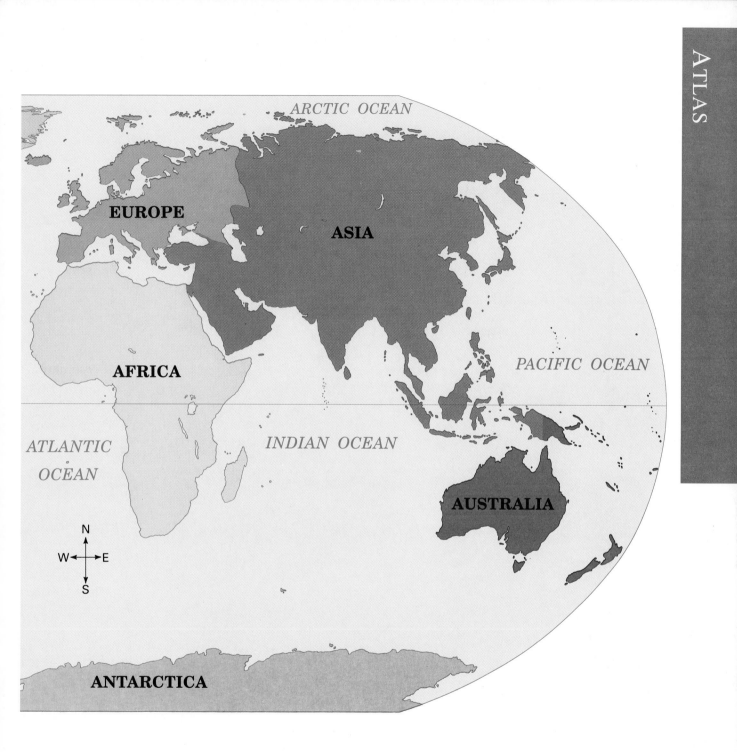

ARCTIC OCEAN

EUROPE

ASIA

AFRICA

PACIFIC OCEAN

INDIAN OCEAN

ATLANTIC
OCEAN

AUSTRALIA

N
W←→E
S

ANTARCTICA

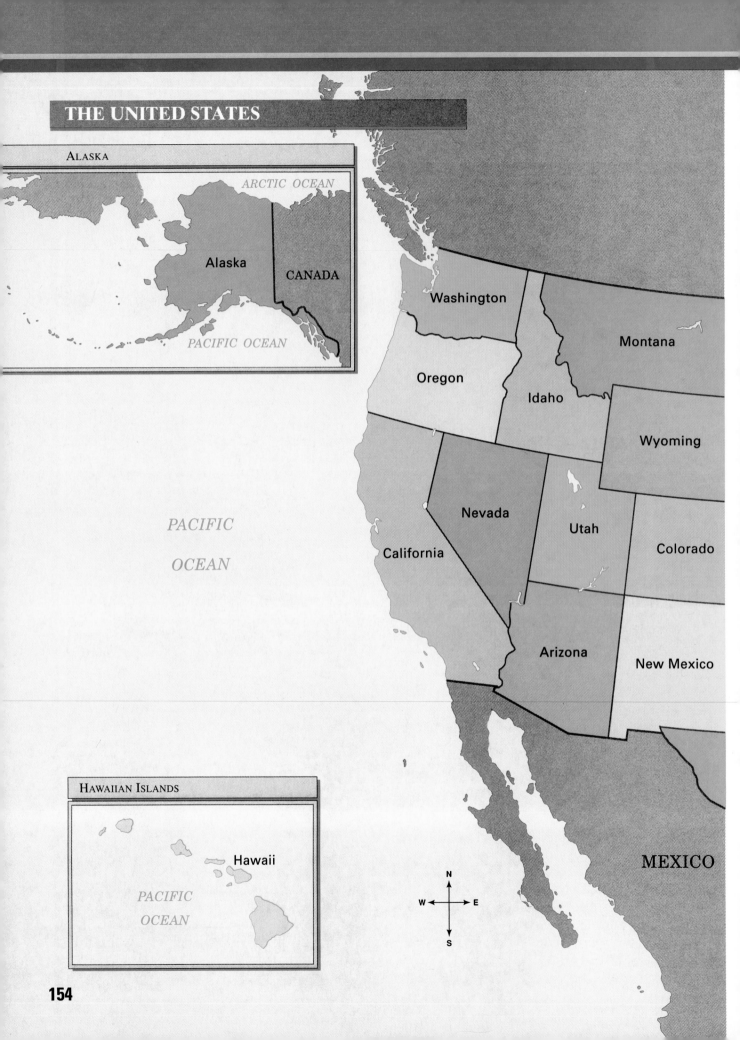

THE UNITED STATES

ALASKA

ARCTIC OCEAN

Alaska

CANADA

PACIFIC OCEAN

Washington

Oregon

Idaho

Montana

Wyoming

Nevada

Utah

Colorado

California

Arizona

New Mexico

PACIFIC

OCEAN

HAWAIIAN ISLANDS

Hawaii

PACIFIC OCEAN

MEXICO

N
W   E
S

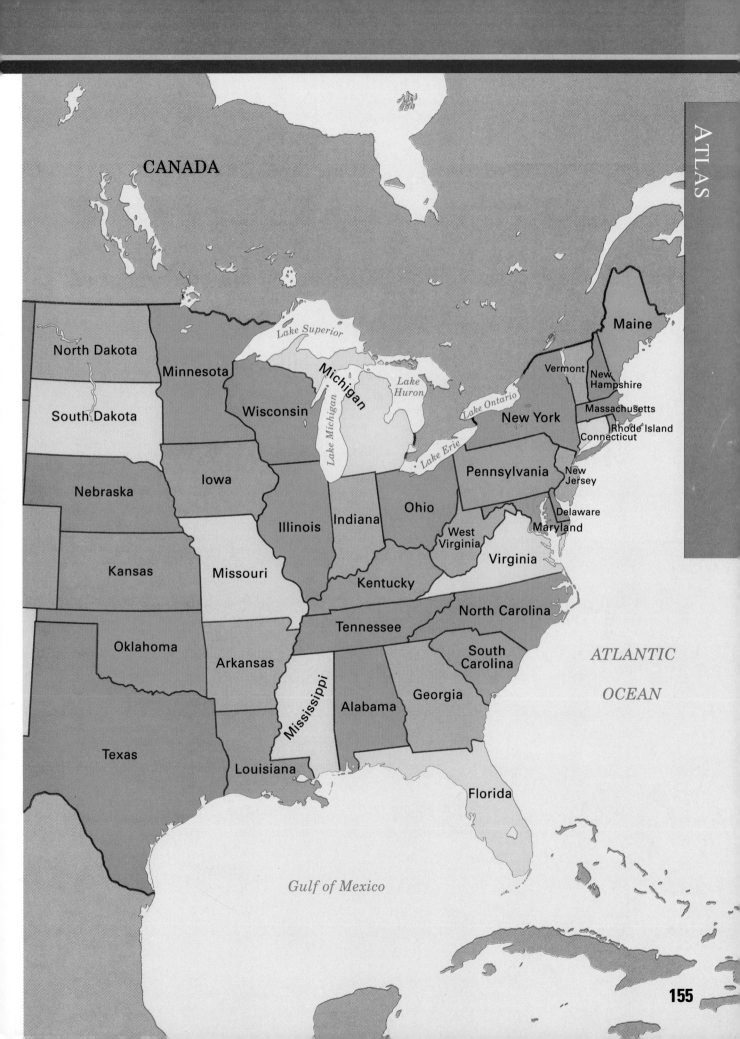

CANADA

Lake Superior

North Dakota

Minnesota

Michigan

Lake Huron

Maine

Vermont

New Hampshire

South Dakota

Wisconsin

Lake Michigan

Lake Ontario

Massachusetts

New York

Rhode Island

Connecticut

Lake Erie

Nebraska

Iowa

Pennsylvania

New Jersey

Illinois

Indiana

Ohio

Delaware

Maryland

West Virginia

Kansas

Missouri

Kentucky

Virginia

ATLANTIC

North Carolina

Tennessee

OCEAN

Oklahoma

Arkansas

South Carolina

Mississippi

Georgia

Texas

Alabama

Louisiana

Florida

Gulf of Mexico

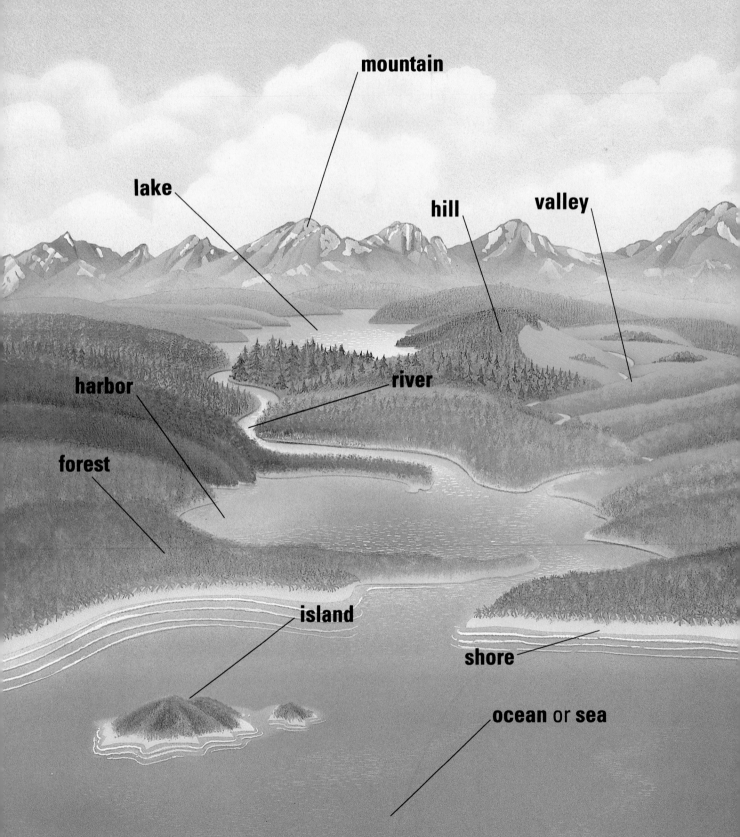

mountain

lake

hill

valley

harbor

river

forest

island

shore

ocean or sea

bar graph

Pets At School

Mice				
Rabbits				
Fish				

page 134

community

page 88

family

page 36

Canada

Canada

page 126

country

United States

page 116

farm

page 42

change

page 90

depend

page 143

farmer

page 54

city

page 68

factory

page 100

flag

page 118

157

friends page 4	**harbor** page 143	**map** page 15
globe page 60	**jobs** page 107	**map key** page 16
goods page 142	**language** page 127	**Mexico** page 136
grow page 31	**link** page 91	**neighborhood** page 30

north

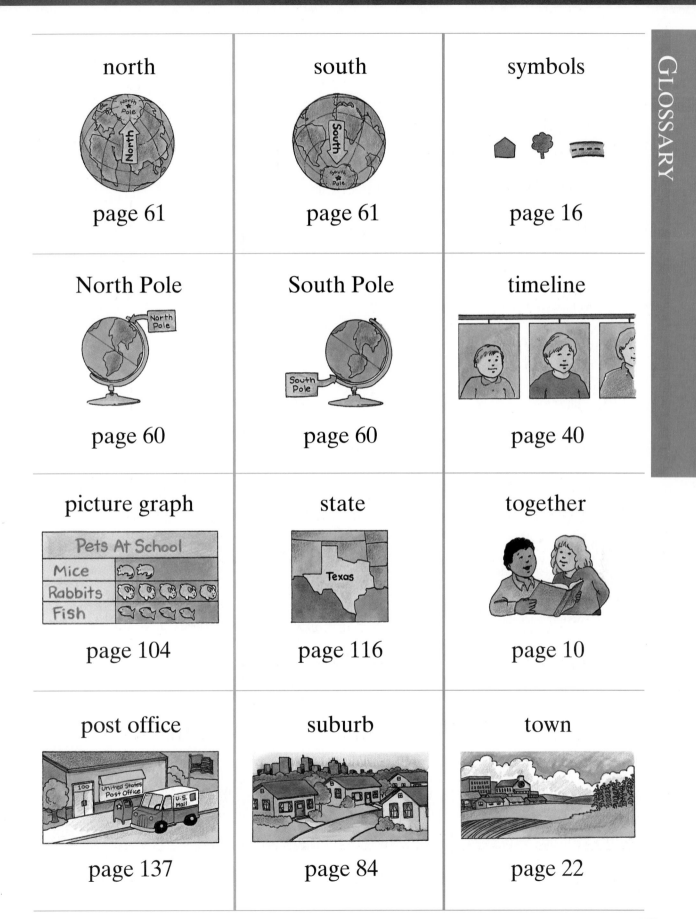

page 61

south

page 61

symbols

page 16

North Pole

page 60

South Pole

page 60

timeline

page 40

picture graph

Pets At School

Mice	
Rabbits	
Fish	

page 104

state

Texas

page 116

together

page 10

post office

U.S. Mail

page 137

suburb

page 84

town

page 22

ACKNOWLEDGMENTS

Text *(continued from page iv)*

46–51 *A Year in the Country* by Douglas Florian. Copyright © 1989 by Douglas Florian. Reprinted by permission of William Morrow & Co. **66** "Skyscraper" by Dennis Lee from *Alligator Pie* by Dennis Lee. Published by Macmillan of Canada. Copyright © 1974 by Dennis Lee. **74–81** *I Go With My Family to Grandma's* by Riki Levinson, illustrated by Diane Goode. Text copyright © 1986 by Riki Levinson. Illustrations © 1986 by Diane Goode. Reprinted by permission of the publisher, Dutton Children's Books a division of Penguin Books USA Inc. **106** "City" by Langston Hughes. Reprinted by permission of Harold Ober Associates Incorporated. Copyright © 1941 by Harper & Bros. Copyright renewed 1969 by Arna Bontemps. **119** "Our Flag" from *Skip Around the Year* by Aileen Fisher. Copyright © 1967 by Aileen Fisher. Reprinted by permission of Harper & Row, Publishers, Inc. **130–33** "Trains" from *Crickety Cricket!* by James S. Tippett. "Trains" originally appeared in *I Go A-Traveling* by James S. Tippett. Text Copyright © 1929 by Harper & Row. Reprinted by permission of Harper & Row, Publishers, Inc. **146–47** "Tugs" from *I Go A-Traveling* by James S. Tippett. Copyright 1929 by Harper & Row, Publishers, Inc. Copyright © 1957 by James S. Tippett. Reprinted by permission of Harper & Row, Publishers, Inc.

Illustrations

Literature border design by Peggy Skycraft.

Ligature 17, 19, 41(b), 61, 91(t), 93(t), 95(t), 105, 113(b), 134, 135, 140–41, 149, 150. **Elizabeth Allen** 22, 23, 24, 25, 26, 27, 28. **Howard Berelson** 110, 111. **Penny Carter** 137. **Brett Cedarholm** 29. **Ray Cruz** 106–7, 108–9. **Susan Dietrich** 34–35, 60. **Steve Edwards** 2, 3, 6, 7. **Len Epstein** 96(b), 97. **Mac Evans** 54, 55, 56, 57, 100, 101, 102, 103. **Ruth Flanigan** 30, 32, 87. **Marla Frazee** 8, 9, 10, 11. **Jackie Geyer** 144–45. **Linda Kelen** 68–69, 70–71, 72–73. **Lorretta Lustig** 42, 43, 44, 45. **Ben Mahan** 142. **Dan McGowan** 156. **Greg McNair** 90–91, 92–93, 94–95, 96. **John Nez** 98, 99. **Larry Nolte** 12, 13, 62(t), 148, 157, 158, 159. **Judy Reed** 82, 83. **Joel Snyder** 104. **Rosiland Soloman** 40, 41(t). **Susan Swan** 66–67. **Fred Winkowski** 14, 15, 16. **Gwynn Wahlmann** 62(b), 63, 112, 113(t). **Other:** 17 Cover illustration from *Mike Mulligan and His Steam Shovel* by Virginia Lee Burton. Copyright 1939 and © 1967 by Virginia Lee Demetrios. Reprinted by permission of Houghton Mifflin Co. **138** Cover illustration from *El Cumpleanos de Spot* by Eric Hill, © 1982 by Eric Hill, reprinted by permission of G. P. Putnam's Sons.

Maps

R. R. Donnelley & Sons Company Cartographic Services 116–17, 152–53, 154–55. **JAK Graphics** 120–21, 126, 136.

Photographs

GH—Grant Heilman Photography; JI—Jeroboam, Inc.; PH—Photographic Resources; PR—Photo Researchers, Inc.; SK—Stephen Kennedy; SM—The Stock Market; TIB—The Image Bank; TS—Tom Stack & Associates

Front cover Peter Bosey. **Back cover** Patricia Caulfield, PR. **xvi–1** © Will and Deni McIntrye, PR. **4** SK (t). Mike Jaeggi (b). **4–5** SK. **5** © Frank Oberle, PH (tl); © Ken Gaghan, JI (tr). © Mel DiGiamcomo, TIB (b). **17** SK. **18** Mike Jaeggi, Meyers Photo-Art (tl,bc); © Alan Cooper, TIB (tc); © Brent Jones (tr,br); © Frank Oberle, PH (bl). **20–21** © Robert Frerck, Odyssey Productions. **28** © R. Perron, Nawrocki Stock Photo. **29** © R. Perron, Nawrocki Stock Photo. **30** Rick Benkof (t); SK (b). **30–31** © Michael Melford, TIB. **31** © John H. Anderson, PH. **32–33** © Larry Lefever, GH. **33** SK. **35** SK. **36** Scott Raffe. **37–38** SK, Erdmann Archive. **39** SK, Erdmann Archive (l); Scott Raffe (r). **40** Mike Phillips, Erdmann Archive. **41** SK. **42** © Larry Lefever, GH (l); © Grant Heilman, GH (r). **43** © Brian Parker, TS (t); © Frank Siteman, JI (b). **44** © Isaac Geib, GH (t); © Grant Heilman, GH (b). **45** © Isaac Geib, GH (l); © Martha Bates, Stock Boston (r). **52** © Grant Heilman, GH (l); SK (tr); © Grant Heilman, GH (cr); © Garry McMichael, GH (br). **53** © Ben Simmons, SM (t); © Robert Frerck, Odyssey Productions (bl); © Ken Love, Nawrocki Stock Photo (bc); SK (br). **54** © Grant Heilman, GH (l); © Larry Lefever, GH (r). **55** © Frank Oberle, PH. **56** © Larry Lefever, GH (t); © Ralston Purina, Battle Creek, MI (b). **57** SK. **58** NASA photo. **59** NASA photo. **60** SK. **61** SK. **64–65** © Barry Lewis, The Network Agency. **68** © John Elk III, Stock Boston. **69** © Greg Vaughn, TS. **70** © Owen Franken, Stock Boston. **71** © Owen Franken, Stock Boston. **72** SK. **73** © Ken Gaghan, JI. **84** SK: SK (cr); © Cameramann International, Ltd. (b). **85** SK: © Brownie Harris, SM (tl); SK (tr,b). **86** SK. **88** © Barry L. Runk, GH (t); © Larry LeFever, GH (b). **89** © Frank Oberle, PH (t); © SM (b). **98** SK. **100** SK (t,r,l); Mike Phillips (b). **101** SK (tl,cr,br); Mike Phillips (tr,bc). **102** SK (tl,br); Mike Phillips (tr,bl). **103** Mike Phillips (t); SK (cl). **104** Mike Phillips. **105** SK (t); © George Hausman, TIB (b). **114–15** © David Barnes, SM. **118–19** © Raphael Macia, PR. **120** © Lowell Georgia, PR (tl); © Suzanne Szasz, PR (cl); © Ilka Hartman, JI (bl); © Loren McIntrye, Woodfin Camp & Associates (bc); © Berlitz, TSW—Click/Chicago Ltd. (br). **120–21** (flags) SK. **121** © J.P. Gobert, PR (t); © Robert Frerck, Woodfin Camp & Associates (b). **122** © John Gerlach, TS (l); © Peter Frank, TSW—Click/Chicago Ltd. (tr); © David W. Hamilton, TIB (br). **123** © Brent Jones (tl); © Superstock (tr); © Dale Jorgenson, TS (bl); © Wernher Krutein, JI (br). **124–25** Ed Book, SM (tl); SK (tr,b). **126** © Suzanne Szasz, PR (t); SK (bl). **126–27** Meyers Photo-Art. **127** SK. **128** © Royal Canadian Mounted Police, Meyers Photo-Art (tl); © Dr. Charles R. Belinky, PR (tr); SK (bl); © Frank Shufletoski, Hot Shots (br). **129** Mitchell B. Reibel, Sportschrome East/West (l); SK (r). **130–33** The Thomas Gilcrease Institute of American History and Art, Tulsa, OK. **134** © Suzanne Szasz, PR. **135** SK. **136** SK. **137** Mike Phillips (tl); © John Chiasson, Gamma-Liason (tr); © Steve Smith (bl); © Mike Jaeggi (br). **138** SK (tl); © Wernher Krutein, JI (c). **138–39** SK. **139** © Steven D. Elmore, TS (l); © Cameramann International, Ltd. (c); © Olof Kallstrom, JI (r). **140** © Roy Morsch, SM (l); © David R. Frazier Photo Library, PR (r). **141** James Blank, SM (tl); SK, U.S. Postal Service (tr); SK (b). **143** © Grant Heilman, GH (t); © Don Murie, Meyers Photo-Art (b). **146–47** © Richard Stockton, PH.

Picture research assistance by Carousel Research, Inc., and Meyers Photo-Art.